Robert Dessaix is and translator. Aft language and literat University of NSW, he presented ABC Radio National's *Books and Writing* program for ten years. In 1995 he began writing full-time. His best-known books are his autobiography *A Mother's Disgrace*, the novels *Night Letters* and *Corfu*, and the travel memoirs *Twilight of Love* and *Arabesques*. He lives in Hobart.

Love   The
Humbug   we
NoRMAN   problem
Anfo   young
              people

Writers in the *On Series*

Robert Dessaix

On Humbug

hachette
AUSTRALIA

Every attempt has been made to locate the copyright holders for material quoted in this book. Any person or organisation that may have been overlooked or misattributed may contact the publisher.

Published in Australia and New Zealand in 2020
by Hachette Australia
(an imprint of Hachette Australia Pty Limited)
Level 17, 207 Kent Street, Sydney NSW 2000
www.hachette.com.au

First published in 2009 by Melbourne University Publishing

10 9 8 7 6 5 4 3 2 1

A catalogue record for this
book is available from the
National Library of Australia

ISBN: 978 0 7336 4390 3 (paperback)

Original cover concept by Nada Backovic Design
Text design by Alice Graphics
Typeset by Typeskill
Printed and bound in Australia by McPherson's Printing Group

The paper this book is printed on is certified against the Forest Stewardship Council® Standards. McPherson's Printing Group holds FSC® chain of custody certification SA-COC-005379. FSC® promotes environmentally responsible, socially beneficial and economically viable management of the world's forests.

The liar has many faces. We misrepresent the facts for the sheer fun of it, to be kind, to be cruel, to boost our self-esteem, to manipulate, to dominate, to enrich ourselves, to avoid punishment and even for artistic reasons. (I fudge and fabricate, after all, every time I write a book, particularly a memoir.) To hoodwink, it seems, is quintessentially human, although it was admittedly a serpent who told the first whopper in the Garden of Eden, not a human being. Lying is evidence of an ability to enter the minds of others, which is why humans and apes can dissemble, but dogs and cows can't. In fact, to tell the truth all the time shows a deplorable *lack* of humanity, and of imagination and respect for the feelings of others.

Kant, it's true, claimed to believe that we have an *absolute* duty not to lie, even if telling the truth should lead to the death of an innocent man, while Montaigne, in a fit of high-mindedness, said that we should pursue lying with fire, such was the horror of it. As a rule, however, it's only very small children who are never untruthful. According to the experts, if your children haven't started lying artfully about once every two hours by the age of four, you're in trouble. It almost certainly means that, like some postmodern theorists, they're failing to distinguish between what is fact and what is fiction. A liar at least recognises the difference. Only dullards, if we are to believe a McGill University survey, fail to start lying creatively and frequently by the age of four. Who wants a four-year-old postmodernist on the loose around the house?

One of the most widespread, and valuable, modes of lying, little commented on, is humbug. The word itself is not very old—it seems to have been in use for less than three hundred years—but it now has a slightly dated ring to it, like 'poppycock', 'piffle', 'baloney' and 'balderdash'. My first memory of hearing the word 'humbug' harks back to reading Dickens's *A Christmas Carol*—or, more likely, to having it read to me. Creeping up on Scrooge in his dingy, cold counting house, his nephew startles him with a cheerful cry of 'A merry Christmas, uncle! God save you!'

'Bah!' says Scrooge, 'Humbug!'

All aglow from walking quickly through the fog, his face 'ruddy and handsome' and his eyes sparkling, his nephew is taken aback. 'Christmas a humbug, uncle!' he says. 'You don't mean that, I am sure.'

But that is precisely what Scrooge means. 'Merry Christmas! What right have you to be merry? What reason have you to be merry? You're poor enough.'

'What right have you to be dismal?' his nephew counters 'gaily'. 'What reason have you to be morose? You're rich enough.'

Having 'no better answer ready on the spur of the moment', Scrooge says 'Bah!' again and follows it up with another 'Humbug'.

This word from the London of Charles Dickens lodged firmly in my mind, together with that dismissive 'Bah!'—and not only in mine, I'm sure, but in the minds of millions of other young readers years ago. Perhaps it's a story less often read to the young these days.

What did Scrooge's use of 'humbug' mean? To wish somebody a Merry Christmas seems harmless enough—harmless almost to the point of meaninglessness. Even 'God save you', while sounding quaint these days, was just a conventional expression of goodwill. So what was Scrooge growling about? He objected to the greeting because, in his curmudgeonly way, he found it impossible to believe that it was a sincere expression of his nephew's true feelings. And that's what humbug does: it makes a show of concocted attitudes and feelings, with little or no semantic thrust. Whether Christmas was, or should be, or could be, a merry affair was beside the point. As far as

Scrooge was concerned, his nephew was an emotional impostor, a humbug.

Humbug is not quite the same as bull-shit, for which it is often mistaken and which has been in the spotlight since Harry G Frankfurt published *On Bullshit* in 2005, and it's not at all the same thing as what is indelicately called mindfucking. All three involve abusing the truth, and all three are rampant in the twenty-first century. However, it is vital to distinguish between them if you want to avoid making a fool of yourself.

It's easy enough to confuse them. In common parlance, for instance, 'bullshit' can refer to almost anything that offends your particular notion of the truth, from the doctrine of the Virgin Birth to Woolworths calling themselves 'the fresh food people', from common and garden poppycock ('I'm resigning to spend more time with my family') to corporate fraud. Yet if we're to negotiate our way with our dignity intact through the veritable bog of untruths surrounding us, we would do well to make a distinction between humbug, bullshit and mindfucking.

In 1835, for instance, the *New York Sun* claimed that the British astronomer Sir John Herschel, by means of a new kind of telescope, had discovered herds of bison, biped beavers and winged men gambolling along the beaches on the moon. Mistaking a classic piece of humbug for the truth, the public was transfixed. A group of Baptist clergymen even held meetings to pray for the moon men's souls. They had no right to feel indignant when the facts of the matter came out, though: nobody likes to be bullshitted, naturally, but the author of the article, Richard Adams Locke, had not been bullshitting them; he had been humbugging them. They had simply mistaken the mode. A century later, no less an intellect than Ludwig Wittgenstein got himself into an unfortunate muddle when a friend who had just had her tonsils out told him that she felt 'just like a dog that has been run over'. Wittgenstein, she said, was 'disgusted', since she could clearly have had no idea of how a run-over dog might feel. In my terms, he took umbrage because he had mistaken harmless humbug for bullshit, as the humourless are inclined to do. The proper response to humbug is to smile or laugh.

Humbug is not just 'bullshit lite', as some commentators seem to suggest. Humbug is a kind of bluster, with a casual disregard for whether something is strictly true or not. If it seeks to mislead at all (and sometimes it can barely be bothered— it's having too much fun), it seeks to play tricks with the speaker's *everyday reality* (situation, attitudes, stance), rather than to deceive anybody with false information, the semantic weight of humbug being pretty much zero. Humbug is more of a disguise than a hoax. Almost every time we say we're sorry, for instance, it's humbug (a ritual display of self-humiliation), as is calling Princess Di 'the people's princess' (she was merely a tragicomic nincompoop at the top of the social pile). Real estate agents' windows are crammed full of humbug, as are, quite properly, most funeral orations and courtroom perorations. The judge's wig is certainly humbug, as is calling him 'your Honour'. Most euphemisms are humbug too: one of the main points of a euphemism is that it does not evoke any mental picture of anything, the words being used having ceased to have any denotative value at all ('surgical strike', 'I'm seeing your sister', 'she's powdering her nose' and so on). Christmas carols are largely humbug, as are transvestism, Marie Antoinette's hamlet at Versailles and all splinters of the True Cross. When Mary

McCarthy said that every word Lillian Hellman wrote was a lie, including 'and' and 'the', she was indulging in humbug. Virtually any reference to 'democracy' is humbug, except in North Korea, where it's bullshit.

Bullshit shares humbug's irreverence for the truth, its semantic negligence, but is uttered in the hope of concealing some other, usually pernicious, truth: the bullshitter's actual enterprise. The bullshitter's aim is not just to disguise this or that tiresome reality (one's actual sex, for instance, or being Queen of France all day, the fact that the corpse was in life a mean-spirited bore or that the only house you can afford will be a dump). Consequently, any mention of the 'war on terror' or 'intelligent design' is probably bullshit, not humbug, and anyone selling chakra balancing or composing a mission statement or writing a reference is almost certainly a bullshitter. Japanese whalers and pro-lifers are bullshitters. (Who isn't pro-life? It's not life they're pro; it's abortion they're anti.) Bullshitters are Greeks bearing gifts. Bullshit is a Trojan horse.

Mindfuckers, as we shall see, operate on a different level again of misrepresentation. Mindfuckers, like lovers or Mormon missionaries, aim to skew your whole psyche.

Perhaps the following experience of mine will help elucidate the differences. A year or so ago in France, I was staying with a friend who had recently bought an antique table. One morning the antique dealer drove up in his smart little van, carried the table into my friend's living room and then stood looking about. The house was a restored medieval building, full of the sort of furniture and knick-knacks that make an old building feel like home. The dealer seemed affable enough, well spoken and anxious to be helpful, if a little too sleek. After a few polite remarks about the view from the window, he paused theatrically and said, 'But you know, I can't help feeling that the feng shui of this room is all wrong'. Humbug, I thought to myself, not believing in force lines you can't measure on a meter and not imagining that a Montpellier antiques dealer with expensive shoes and a Parisian accent would either. Surely monsieur was just indulging in a bit of playful persiflage to pass the time? My friend, for her part, seemed mildly intrigued. He then began to poke about a bit, telling her to get rid of the buddha on the mantelpiece (it was 'poisoning' the room), to replace the picture on the staircase of ducks swooping downwards with one of ducks swooping upwards ('otherwise you risk a fall') and to do something about the heavy, black beams in the ceiling because they were radiating oppressive negative energy throughout the house. Bullshit, I thought. What's his game? Oddly enough, my friend, usually so rational, so Presbyterian, seemed curious. Then he produced his card and said, 'You know, I run classes on feng shui in

town—I think you might find them inter-
esting. As a matter of fact, I've got a course
starting the week after next. Give me a call
if you'd like to join us'. I don't believe this,
I thought to myself. This isn't bullshit, it's
a *mindfuck*. (I'd been reading *Mindfucking*
by Colin McGinn, so the word sprang to
mind. Say what you like, it's got a certain
punch.)

I'd had enough. 'I might go upstairs
and read a book', I said. Neither my friend
nor the antiques dealer really noticed.
It's true that I stumbled on the stairs and
bruised a knee, but there was a perfectly
rational explanation for that. Pictures of
ducks swooping downwards had nothing
to do with it.

Humbug litters everyday intercourse. I took the antique dealer's first remark about feng shui to be humbug because it struck me as just a bit of innocuous banter signifying nothing, little more than an attempt to put himself in character, as it were. Theatre—that's all it was, I thought. Prattle. Humbug. I didn't imagine that he *meant* anything by it. He might just as well have said, 'I can't help feeling that the feng shui of this room is perfect'. It would have made just as much sense and still been humbug.

If the world is awash with humbug, it's just as well it is. Without it, our lives would be drab affairs indeed. There's a lot of bullshit around as well, and a considerable measure of mindfucking, but humbug is indistinguishable from the air we breathe. It starts with 'Good morning!', continues through 'Excuse me!' and 'How are you?' and ends with 'Good night!' In the Middle East it pops up regularly throughout the day as 'God willing'. It threads its way harmlessly through our routine conversations, less innocently through the vapid twaddle of our politicians and the advertisements we read and see on television. On occasion it can become quite brazen: at many public events in Australia, for instance, it pops up in the form of 'acknowledging the traditional owners of the land' before the festivities get underway. What on earth a phrase such as this could *mean* is anybody's guess—much the same, I suspect, as the 'Love' we put at the end of letters to people we clearly do not love or a line or two of 'I like Aeroplane jelly'. Like most instances of humbug, from best-selling novels to blather about democracy, this piece of fake piety positions itself to take advantage of current vanities and conceits.

In short, humbug is not unlike a pink party wig: the wig is not a statement about your hair colour; it's just an expression of your desire to disguise your everyday reality in particular surroundings. A toupee is another matter altogether: a party wig is fake while a toupee is false. This is a subtle distinction worth bearing in mind.

Humbug's connotation is often of phoniness or sideshow flim-flammery with a tacky edge—even of kitsch. What, apart from the recent papal visit to Australia, could be more kitsch than a pink party wig, after all? A wig may not be vulgarly sentimental in quite the way that 'The Dying Swan' or souvenir-shop boomerangs are, but it *is* an instance of shameless pretence, a declaration of feelings and character thought to be appropriate in the circumstances, whether genuinely felt or not. Crap, in vernacular terms, like an obviously fake Rolex, rather than bullshit. It's what the film critic in *The Times* was alluding to when he called the film *Australia* 'a quite extraordinary piece of kitsch'. 'No one in their right mind', he went on, 'would describe [it] as great art. It's fabulous popcorn: a vintage, life-affirming weepy that begs you to turn off your brain and ogle at the spectacular views'. Peter Conrad in the *Monthly* dismissed Baz Luhrmann's epic in similar terms, calling it 'giddy, garbled, retrograde kitsch'. Exactly the sort of thing that Scrooge would have greeted with 'Bah! Humbug!'

In America, humbug is probably more closely associated with figures from the Jacksonian era such as PT Barnum ('The Greatest Show on Earth') than with Charles Dickens's Scrooge. Between Andrew Jackson's election to the presidency in 1828 and the Civil War, there was a blossoming of huckstering in America: it was the era (like our own) of the self-made man selling questionable goods by questionable means to an educated, but credulous, public—credulous because sceptical about almost everything except its own ability to sniff out deception, every man and woman according to his or her individual judgement. Quintessentially capitalist and very Protestant. Given the parallels with our own times, it is unsurprising that sniffing out—the very process of uncovering trickery, roguery or plotted deception of any kind, especially of the criminal variety—is flourishing again today. Our present fascination with the crime genre, as well as with 'the mystery of the pyramids' (the Sphinx, the Aztecs, the Maya and so on), has its origins in that very same era in American and English fiction: the era of Edgar Allan Poe and Conan Doyle.

Barnum moved on quickly from sharp business practices to showmanship, where humbug can always be seen in its purest, most enjoyable light. Even the vast mansion he eventually built himself was humbug: it was a turreted, oriental fantasy called Iranistan set in pleasure gardens in Bridgeport, Connecticut. Pure puffery. As is the case today in Western or Westernised countries, learning gave way to entertainment, drama to melodrama, and enlightenment to fun and games in Jackson's more 'democratic' (that is, individualistic) America, with museums becoming amusement centres and the media peddling sensation as much as news. Living statues (humbug incarnate) came into fashion, as they've done in our own cities in recent years, along with ventriloquists, automatons, impersonators and 'curiosities' of every description. The point was not whether Barnum's 'Fejee mermaid' with her fish's body and monkey's hands and head, his 'Tom Thumb', his 'Irish giant', his trained fleas, fat boys, bearded ladies and dwarves were *really* monsters, but that they were intriguing, they were fun. It was of no account whether Jenny Lind, the 'Swedish nightingale' with 'a voice like a sister's kiss', was *really* a stupendously gifted singer and the incarnation of moral virtue and artlessness; the show was real; the public hysteria when she arrived in the United States was real and made both Barnum and Lind rich.

All these 'curiosities' and celebrities tested your credulity in the context of a carnival. In fact, when Joice Heath, whom Barnum exhibited as George Washington's 161-year-old nurse, eventually stopped pulling in the crowds, he himself wrote a letter to the local newspaper suggesting that she was a fraud, a 'curiously constructed automaton, made up of whale bone, India-rubber, and numberless springs'. He once even arranged for someone to prosecute him for imposture on the grounds that his American Museum's bearded lady was a man. In other words, the truth was immaterial to Barnum. It was all about the show. All Barnum wanted to do, quite openly, was to give pleasure to the masses and make a lot of money. (Well, everyone's peddling *something*, after all.) When an English tourist to his museum asked him if the displays were real or humbug, he replied, 'That's just the question: persons who pay their money at the door have a right to form their own opinions after they have got up the stairs'. What Barnum understood was that humbug should *never* be unquestionable. Only bullshitters and mindfuckers (and liars, of course) find questions unnerving.

Whether or not an utterance or act is humbug never depends on its truthfulness. The whole point about humbug is precisely that truthfulness is beside the point: you don't just not mean what you say; you don't even quite know what you mean—you're just clowning around. Is

Pepsi *really* 'the one'? How exactly would you go about determining whether it was or wasn't? The point is to become almost unhinged with excitement at the prospect of drinking a beverage that tastes, as the comic strip *Bloom County* once put it, 'like malted battery acid'. What you say may indeed be codswallop, claptrap or cock-and-bull, for instance, or hot air, hokum and hogwash; it may even be gibberish, like the doctrine of the Trinity or astrological predictions (that is to say, unclarifiably implausible)—the English language is rich in terms for calling something nonsense—but it will only be humbug if you not only don't care whether it's tosh or not, but don't really give two hoots about whether you're believed or not.

Like the television newsreader who wishes you, on behalf of the entire news team, a great weekend, the perpetrator of humbug is only concerned about acting out a part with flair, not about what is being said. You're not being seriously swindled, any more than the reader of science fiction (enjoyable humbug) or the singer of a national anthem (more sinister humbug) is. In PT Barnum's phrase, it's just social therapy.

If, for example, just for a lark, an overweight father of three in his fifties posts a raunchy story on an Internet porn site giving the impression that he is a 23-year-old sexual livewire called Jed looking for action, then he's guilty of nothing more than humbug. He's just a japer.

This is pink wig territory. Anyone who emails back with a proposition, hoping for a steamy night or two with a rascally tomcat, has made a category mistake. If, on the other hand, he places a personal ad in a singles magazine, advertising himself (as people do in the *New York Review of Books* every fortnight) as a spunky, warm-hearted, intellectually curious leader in the arts who is passionate about politics, tapas in Barcelona, Mozart sonatas, Japanese ceramics, and snuggling by the fire reading Heidegger, then he is guilty of bullshit. It may all be more or less true, at least in his own mind: he may indeed run a book group on the first Tuesday in the month, have enjoyed a visit to a tapas bar in Barcelona in 1970 and once flicked through *Being and Time* with at least Tchaikovsky playing in the background. If you don't look too closely, the wooden horse may look vaguely like a real one. Now, though, he is hiding another truth behind the up-market blather: he is fifty-seven, married and very much the worse for wear. And, more importantly, he is concealing the true nature of his enterprise: to inveigle an attractive young sophisticate into an affair with a nobody. This is akin to what journalists in the *Australian* do when they carry on about the 'free market', which exists on the same level of reality as Cinderella, or cornered politicians when they claim they can't recall what happened: they are obscuring their true enterprise behind bursts of hot air. Moralists calling for the prosecution of Bill Henson for his supposedly disgusting photographs are doing much the same thing. The French antiques dealer, in advising my friend to get rid of the buddha on the mantelpiece, is guilty of the same act of concealment. Maybe the buddha is pestiferous; maybe it isn't—he is in no position to know either way and can scarcely be expected to care. The buddha is simply serving as a wooden horse, his real concern now being to keep my friend focused on it while he marshals the troops he's hidden inside. This is no longer mere banter: like the journalists in the *Australian*, the amnesiac politicians and those calling for the Henson photographs to be banned, his interest is not in what is true or untrue but in winning compliance with a hidden agenda. And that is bullshitting. That's toupee territory.

The two modes obviously overlap. Since it is not the meaning of what is said or enacted that is important—not the semantic aspect so much as the pragmatic effect—whether we regard something as humbug or bullshit will usually depend on who is producing it and in what context. If, for instance, a politician rabbits on about 'democracy' while making an election speech, it will almost certainly be just humbug, on the same semantic level as kissing babies or smiling for the camera. He may as well be singing 'Jingle Bells'. After all, nobody has the faintest idea what 'democracy' might usefully mean in the modern world—it tends to mean little more than some form of the parliamentary system. 'Democracy' in that sense is a word like 'God' or expressions such as 'freedom of speech' or 'Oh, what a feeling! Toyota!' We do know what it doesn't mean, of course, which narrows the field, but not much: it doesn't mean military dictatorship, for instance, or Stalinist totalitarianism, just as 'God' doesn't normally mean a garden hose or a box of chocolates. (Pantheists might disagree.) However, when the regime in North Korea or the Democratic Republic of Congo calls itself 'democratic', we rightly suspect bullshit. In this context the use of the word 'democratic' is not just a matter of calling the *7.30 Report* interviewer 'mate' (as Peter Garrett likes to do) or reciting the Lord's

Prayer at the opening of a parliamentary session (humbug before the bullshit begins), but an attempt to cover up political realities that could in no sense be called 'democratic' to the benefit of these countries' rulers. Its usage is no longer just a good-natured practical joke, as it is when an Australian or British prime minister resorts to it. It is now bullshit.

At a more trivial level, the horoscope column in my local newspaper is (to me) an example of mere humbug, a few lines of entertaining flummery, a spot of codswallop providing me with a moment or two of hilarity over breakfast. Once it enters the realm of quackery, however, as it does sometimes in the pages of certain women's magazines or on certain websites, attempting to extract profit from the ped-dling of gobbledygook as truth, it veers towards bullshit. (In the worst cases, where complete and permanent bamboozlement is the aim, a concerted effort being made to relocate the whole mind-set of the prey in la-la land, the purveyors of astrology are indistinguishable from mindfuckers.)

The most oft-quoted example of bull-shit in recent American discussions of it is the reasons given for the war in Iraq. In fact, in *Bullshit and Philosophy*, a col-lection of philosophers' essays edited by Gary L Hardcastle and George A Reisch in response to Frankfurt's *On Bullshit*, the editors suggest in their introduc-tion that it was the bullshit surrounding the war in Iraq that made the discussion

of bullshit so 'very apropos for today'.
The essayists in *Bullshit and Philosophy*
return again and again to the example of
George Bush's stated reasons for invading
Iraq and his 'war on terror'. 'Bullshit', as
Reisch himself writes, 'is being informed
that this dictator possesses nuclear weapons and soon plans to use them on allies
and neighboring nations'. This is bullshit
because whether or not Saddam Hussein
had these weapons and planned to use
them was of little or no concern to Bush
and his allies: their reason for invading
was unconnected to whether he did or
didn't. They didn't actually even know
the truth of the matter, despite all their
spies and intelligence agencies, although
every second taxi-driver in Melbourne did

know, I remember, and correctly predicted the outcome of any invasion. The important thing was to conceal the real reason or reasons for the invasion, as it always is for a bullshitter. Indeed, in grand bullshitting style, when the untruth of the WMD accusations became too obvious for even Bush and Blair to keep repeating, they flailed about for a bit and then came up with a fresh load of bullshit, as bullshitters typically do: we were really invading Iraq to restore something called 'freedom and democracy'. Whatever the reasons were that led the Bush administration to make the catastrophic decision to invade Iraq, we can be certain that the restoration of freedom and democracy to Iraq was not foremost among them. Even if we believe that the war was justified, as some intelligent, thoughtful people clearly do, the reasons given for launching it were classic bullshit.

Politics, along with advertising and the PR industry, is a rich field for bullshit detectives, but there is also a widespread antagonism among writers on bullshit (and humbug—even philosophers often confuse the two) to religion. From professional philosophers such as Max Black in *The Prevalence of Humbug and Other Essays* and most of the contributors to *Bullshit and Philosophy*, to the journalist and broadcaster Francis Wheen in *How Mumbo-Jumbo Conquered the World* and Laura Penny in *Your Call Is Important to Us: The Truth About Bullshit*, commentators on humbug and bullshit regularly and with relish pounce on examples taken from religion to illustrate their cases. At this point in history few are likely to single out Islam or Judaism for ridicule, while Buddhism in Western countries, perhaps because it presents itself as a 'way of life' rather than as a religion or truth narrative, seems to attract little criticism, so Christianity is the religion they usually target.

The hostility to religion is so consistent that one of the editors of *Bullshit and Philosophy*, Gary L Hardcastle, Assistant Professor of Philosophy at Bloomsburg University in Pennsylvania, feels compelled in his own essay to point out that much of the opposition to bullshit 'comes from a notion of "science" as truth', so, naturally enough, what riles these commentators is any hint of metaphysics, represented from their logical positivist point of view by meaningless terms such as 'the Infinite', 'God', 'principle' and so on. Religious systems of belief—even a belief in a Supreme Being—are not necessarily irrational *in themselves*: they are irrational only from the standpoint of other truths. (This is a big 'only' in the early twenty-first century, but an important one.) Of course, what makes any religious belief, rational or irrational, humbug or bullshit is not its implausibility or absurdity according to commonly held notions of how reality is configured—the Virgin Birth, say, reincarnation or any of the Aboriginal creation stories are all at variance with modern, scientific notions—but its function when articulated. The story of the ancestral being Guthi-guthi, for example, banging on a mountain to let Weowie the water spirit out, thereby creating the streams and waterholes around Mount Grenfell, may be complete mumbo jumbo to me, every detail of my daily life being predicated on the conviction that geographical features are produced by other forces entirely, but that doesn't make the story itself either humbug or bullshit. The story is not even irrational *in itself*: it is only irrational to me because I connect the streams and waterholes around Mount Grenfell to another, incompatible story: the scientific one. And, to be fair, we all constantly bracket off sets of beliefs about what is true and what is not, ignoring their incompatibility. We simply can't be sure, with our limited understanding of how the universe works, that they will ultimately prove to be incompatible. Tony Blair, for instance, for all his apparent rationality, seems to believe that the wine in his communion cup is the actual blood of a Jewish man who died 2000 years ago; the widely respected French philosopher Luce Irigaray believes that Einstein's $E=mc^2$ equation privileges the speed of light over 'less masculine speeds', and Air Vice Marshal Sir Peter Horsley, Oxford-educated and once deputy commander-in-chief of Strike Command in Great Britain,

was convinced he'd met an extraterres-
trial being named Janus while working at
Buckingham Palace. I myself knew a brain
surgeon who believed that his cat was tele-
pathic. My high-school maths teacher,
a man of alarming intelligence, believed
that he was receiving messages from Mars
in his inner-spring mattress every night.
They all live (or lived) happily in a world
that functions on the understanding that
these beliefs must be hogwash, incompatible with the truths that reasonably explain
the observable universe. They are or were
bracketing—as we all do when it suits us.

Religious beliefs are most commonly
encountered by the nonbeliever as humbug, at least in a Christian context, during

the rituals of christening, marriage and burial, as well as in the now rather old-fashioned exchanges of the 'God bless you!' type: in the twenty-first century, these ceremonies and greetings are little more than ritualised polite banter, and serve a useful social purpose. They become bullshit, however, if we suspect that the speaker, while caring little about the truthfulness of his utterance, is trying to conceal and win our complicity with another agenda. Religious assertions can hardly, after all, be shown to be either true or false. The Creator of the universe may or may not approve of homosexuality, for instance. Who is to know? To assert that He does not, however, is less likely to arouse hostility, especially in Kansas or

Casablanca, than the admission that you find sexual enjoyment with anyone except a legal spouse a threat to public order, not to mention to your own sexual arrangement.

It was instructive to read the reasons given by an Islamic authority in Algeria for his concern about the recent spate of conversions of Muslims in his country to Christianity. Proselytising to convert Muslims to other religions is banned by the Algerian Constitution, although conversion to Islam, needless to say, is perfectly legal. However, conversions to Christianity are taking place at such a rate in the region of Kabylia, a Berber stronghold, that even the churches themselves are concerned by the possibility of a violent reaction against their members. 'We shouldn't kill one another in the name of religion', the Algerian Religious Affairs Minister told the newspaper *Liberté*. 'That people come from the US and France to spread ideas contrary to national unity— that's the danger.' That, it seems to me, is not bullshit. I happen to value freedom of conscience over national unity, but I have no cause to dismiss the minister's remarks as bullshit. The Algerian government has enough problems already in Kabylia with Islamic militants regularly committing mass atrocities as part of their campaign to overthrow the government, so the last thing Algeria needs is Berbers, who already nurture a longstanding, deep-seated hostility to Arabisation, arming themselves with another pretext for undermining the country's unity (such as it is).

In neighbouring Morocco, however, where proselytising to convert a Muslim is also illegal, public statements of opposition do have a whiff of bullshit about them. Here the number of recent converts is much more modest, although still disturbing, and the conversions are overwhelmingly of Berbers to Protestant denominations. The Roman Catholic Archbishop Vincent Landel has complained that the conversions 'upset everything' because 'all these evangelical converts lack restraint and discretion—they do any old thing'. The General Secretary of the Superior Council of Ulemas,

Mohammed Yssef, takes a different tack: he claims to object to the conversions on the grounds that they are unethical, exploiting as they do 'people with a weak understanding of their own religion ... the poor and the sick' and Berbers who have failed to understand that Islam is not a religion imposed by the Arabs but 'the religion of God ... neither Arab nor Berber'. Bullshit. What both these men are hiding behind a cloud of blather is another, less acceptable truth: they don't like losing their control over the lives of others.

Religion also provides an excellent gateway to the world of mindfucking. The mindfucker, it must be remembered, is in an entirely different league from the humble humbug or crafty bullshitter. Whereas bullshit is always objectionable—nobody, as Colin McGinn points out in *Mindfucking*, wants to be bullshitted—mindfucking can be either positive or negative. Whichever it is, in its power and complexity its abuse of the truth reaches far beyond the limits of humbug or bullshit. A mindfucker wants to manipulate others to think and behave as he wishes them to over an extended period of time—'forever', in the case of lovers. He wishes to permanently reconfigure another's whole psyche for his own gain, as Scrooge's nephew or even George Bush did not.

If the term seems uncomfortably crass—even if we are becoming inured to what JC in the *Times Literary Supplement* delights in calling 'the FCUK-isation of everything'—it is also peculiarly appropriate, at least according to McGinn's formulation of what mindfucking is. As he describes it in his slim study of the subject, it is indeed analogous to a life-changing erotic experience. In fact, McGinn suggests that falling in love may be one of the best examples we have of being mindfucked. Besides, there is really no other single term in English that covers this multifaceted phenomenon quite as effortlessly and succinctly, as well as picturesquely, as 'mindfucking'.

'Brainwashing', for instance, which comes close in certain contexts, is normally used in a negative sense and of organisations rather than individuals. Oppressive regimes are said to brainwash their citizens, interrogators to brainwash their victims on behalf of their masters, and fast-food companies to brainwash whole swathes of the population through advertising and promotional schemes. Religious organisations, many might say, brainwash the young through their school systems and anyone else they can get their hands on through a variety of manipulatory means, from managed hysteria on a massive scale, such as World Youth Day, to retreats in Indian ashrams. Whether the ideology or world view or even dietary regime is in itself bunkum is beside the point: it is irrelevant whether the pope is the Vicar of Christ or merely an ageing German with delusions of grandeur, whether the people and the Party really were 'one' (as the banners in

Moscow used to assure us in Soviet times) or scarcely related, or whether a certain set of French theories—for argument's sake, let's say French poststructuralist theories, which strike many of us as being a mixture of the bleeding obvious and impenetrable tripe—have anything plausible to say about how to decode our experience. The point about brainwashing is rather that certain organisations—religious institutions, corporations, governments, academic elites and so on—are attempting to restructure our outlook on life in a fundamental and (they would hope) long-term way, usually without rational persuasion. They want you to embrace their theories as truths and live your life accordingly.

The term 'mindfucking', however, is more expansive: it covers both institutional brainwashing and the engineering of a change in somebody's psyche by another individual, even when reason is used as a tool. Einstein and Freud once changed the way we looked at the world, of course, and through rational persuasion; on a more trivial level today, some might say that Kylie Minogue and André Ricu, with the aid of gigantic publicity machines, are still skewing minds in the area of musical taste. However, since they were or are individuals, not establishments, and since the worst any of them has done is turn our brains to pulp, we are unlikely to say that they have 'brainwashed' us. They have all, however, mindfucked us, sometimes usefully, often pleasurably.

Ideological mindfuckers, unlike the promoters of mere tastes, are usually intent on convincing us that someone else has already mindfucked us, but erroneously. Marxists pitted their ideology against established bourgeois consciousness; postmodernists have attacked 'science' and its totalising tendencies as manufactured knowledge, mere social process; logical positivists deplore the pervasive influence of metaphysics on our thinking; creationists see Darwinism as an atheist plot to undermine Christianity; and some Republicans see socialised medicine as a Communist conspiracy.

Individuals can rarely mindfuck us without backup—even Kylie has a team behind her. When they do, eros is almost always playing a part, which is why 'mindfucking' is a term that really does hit the nail on the head when it comes to describing enduring mind-changing manipulation. In the twenty-first century, one-on-one possession (a word that itself has erotic overtones, of course) is unlikely to take place without sexual sway of some kind being exerted. Most of the modern words for this kind of controlling influence (indoctrination, persuasion, re-education, exploitation) do not connote a sexual component, but some of the older words do: beguile, bewitch, enthral, enchant, enrapture, spellbind and, more distantly, hex, voodoo and mesmerise. Whether it is a spouse, a lover, a cult leader or even a schoolteacher who reconfigures the way you think, sexual magnetism, banishing reason, is almost certain to play some role in the transformation.

Falling in love feels like being mind-fucked (rational thought flies out the window; you are possessed by irrational urges; the entire universe from your breakfast cereal to the meaning of life appears in a new light) but in this instance you may, of course, be mindfucking yourself. Like a religious epiphany, however, where reason is suddenly flooded out by a whole symphonic wave of emotion and primal perceptions, falling in love rarely induces a permanent state: after the initial *coup de foudre*, it generally morphs into something more comfortable, if still beyond reason. This raises the complex question of self-deception in the whole discussion of humbug, bullshit and mindfucking: can we indeed single-handedly deceive ourselves? And if so, what exactly is going on? The humbug is not deceiving anyone, so here the question doesn't arise. But in the case of bullshit and mindfucking, can one part of the mind overpower another, conceal information from another? The philosopher Max Black in his book *The Prevalence of Humbug and Other Essays* argues that, strictly speaking, self-deception is an impossibility: you either believe something or you don't. You either believe that you're the Duchess of Marlborough or you don't. You can't believe that you're really the Duchess of Marlborough *and* really a checkout girl in Bundaberg at one and the same time. Or can you? Maybe not at one and the same time, but episodically perhaps you can. It may be difficult to bullshit yourself, although many politicians and priests appear to succeed at it, darting in and out of fantasy land repeatedly every day, but as anyone who has fallen in love one-sidedly or seen the Virgin Mary in a piece of toast knows, you can most certainly mindfuck yourself. You're not quite as unitary as you think you are.

In short, whereas humbug and bull-shit both involve imposture either for play or to conceal another truth or enterprise, the mindfucker aims not just to create a false impression about himself for his own limited purposes, but to reconfigure your entire psyche. The effect can be both benign and malign. Learning Bulgarian, for example, will reconfigure your psyche and in that sense be a mindfuck: a delicious one if you're doing it for fun, say, or are an Australian married to a Bulgarian, but if you'd been a member of the Turkish minority in Bulgaria during the Communist years, it might have felt less benign. Scientology, I tend to believe, began life as a creative writing exercise (harmless humbug), soon turned profitable as bullshit and ended up as a mindfuck of gigantic proportions. Mormonism, I suspect, went through much the same process, starting

out as a bit of childish humbug on Joseph
Smith's part (a little fantasy about angelic
visitants in a forest in Wayne County, New
York—well, he was only fourteen at the
time, and it was 1820, so pretending to
be Batman wasn't an option), turned into
bullshit with Smith's claim to have discovered gold plates inscribed in Ancient
Egyptian in 1827 and then burgeoned into
a major mindfuck in about 1830 with the
formation of the Church of Jesus Christ
of Latter-Day Saints, now a worldwide
organisation governing the lives of millions. PT Barnum, charitably looking on
Mormonism as just humbug, told Brigham
Young, Smith's successor, that he consid-
ered him 'the best show in America' and

wanted to tour him along with Chang and Eng the Siamese twins and an entourage of midgets, but by the 1870s Mormonism was no longer just a circus.

Mormonism is a benign mindfuck from the point of view of Mormons, even many educated Mormons who don't quite swallow in their entirety the extraordinary doctrines of their organisation, but a malign one from the point of view of the *Catholic Encyclopedia*, for example. On the subject of Catholicism, much the same thing could no doubt be said of the Fatima episode: three Portuguese shepherd children in 1917 concoct a few encounters with the Blessed Virgin to while away the time, elaborating on familiar stories as children do (as I did myself in my own backyard, although in my case it was usually something by Enid Blyton); it's taken up and turned into bullshit by those who can have no idea of the facts of the matter since the message was inherently unclarifiable, but who recognise a publicity opportunity for their endeavour when they see one; and then it becomes a mindfuck, with millions captivated by the narrative, benignly or embarrassingly, depending on your point of view. Like Salt Lake City, Utah, Fatima in Portugal is doing very nicely out of the transformation.

If you want to sharpen your wits to identify a mindfuck, it's useful to keep an eye out for the following signs: a disinclination to engage in rational persuasion (not true of Einstein, Marx or Darwin, of course, but commonly true) with an appeal to the emotions above reason; an enthusiasm for what McGinn calls 'informational isolation' (the closed borders and censorship of the Soviet bloc, the enclosed nature, even physical isolation, of many sects and cults); the insistence on the unity of the message; a demand for trust; and a tendency to keep those inside in a state of fear and loathing vis-à-vis those outside (the West, socialists, the criminal classes and so on). The parallels with romantic love, not to mention with the tabloid press and *A Current Affair*, are obvious: you 'fall under a spell'; your reason takes a holiday; your psyche becomes an overheated brazier of dreams, desires and resentments; you want to be intimately alone with whoever has cast the spell; you start collecting stamps or watching old John Wayne movies because your beloved likes to do that; you see enemies and rivals everywhere; you live for a repeat of the epiphanic moment; you become an emotional wreck; you surrender; you say 'yes' to everything; you become deaf and blind; you start living out borrowed narratives; you are in love. It's all quite fabulous, of course, and definitely not to be missed.

It's mindfucking I began to suspect that the French antiques dealer was aiming for, just before I stumbled upstairs. Once he came up with the offer of a feng shui course in Montpellier, I had the distinct feeling that he was no longer just prattling on with a bit of friendly humbug, or inveigling my friend into trusting him to redecorate her living room with a bit of waffling bullshit about poison buddhas and swooping ducks, but was actually now intent on locking her into a mind-set he could exploit at leisure—mindfucking her, in other words. For the record, she did not sign up.

'We live in an era of unprecedented bull-shit production', Penny writes on the first page of *Your Call Is Important to Us*. 'Never in the history of mankind have so many people uttered statements that they know to be untrue. Presidents, priests, politicians, lawyers, reporters, corporate executives, and countless others have taken to saying not what they actually believe, but what they want others to believe—not what is, but what works.' (For them, that is.) 'Unprecedented', 'Never in the history of mankind'—these are strong words. Can they be true? Frankfurt, too, writes about the 'contemporary proliferation of bullshit', although he concedes that 'it is impossible to be sure that there is relatively more of it nowadays than at other times', while in *How Mumbo-Jumbo Conquered the World*, Wheen argues that a sort of 'Voodoo Revolution' has taken place: in 1979, when Margaret Thatcher came to power in the United Kingdom and the Ayatollah Khomeini turned Iran back into a medieval theocracy, the Enlightenment was shunted off into the wings. For the last quarter of a century or so, according to Wheen, we've been living in a world where poppycock (postmodern theories, New Age loonies, creationists, astrologers, swindlers and mob hysteria) rules supreme.

All these commentators gaily confuse humbug, bullshit and mindfucking as if the difference were of no more account than that between Guinea and Guinea Bissau. It's understandable: on a world scale, the difference is insignificant and they *are* contiguous. Who cares about subtle differences, you might object, in an era marked by the Enron (and now Madoff) collapses, the paedophile scandals in the Roman Catholic Church, eBay fraud, multiple literary hoaxes and the latest US electoral campaign (a veritable extravaganza of humbug, bullshit and mindfucking)? I think that getting the terminology right does matter. Without doing this we can't think clearly about what we should defend ourselves against (and how to do it) and what we should just lie back and enjoy.

Take the Frey case, for example. A few years ago, a young alcoholic and drug-abuser called James Frey hawked around a novel about a young alcoholic drug-abuser that had an inspiring ending. No publisher was interested. So it was marketed instead in 2003 as a memoir. Amazon.com selected it as their favourite book of 2003; the *New Yorker* described it as a 'frenzied, electrifying description of the experience', and Frey and his publishers did very nicely out of the exercise. Right from the beginning, awkward questions were raised, notably by the *Minneapolis Star Tribune*, about the factual nature of some of the incidents in the book. (Frey claimed to have been gaoled for eighty-seven days at one point, for instance, whereas records showed that he had been merely held at a police station for five hours.) In 2006, *Smoking Gun* alleged that large parts of the memoir had been fabricated. Frey appeared on *Larry King Live*, defending his book as a memoir, saying (quite rightly) that memoirs often alter details for literary effect. In my terms, he was arguing that a little humbug—a spot of fluff to round out the

corners and give shape to a shapeless life—
is permissible in literature, and a memoir
is literature. As he wrote himself in a note
for later editions of the book, 'I wanted the
stories in the book to ebb and flow, to have
dramatic arcs, to have the tension that all
great stories require'.

No lesser personage than Oprah
Winfrey happened to catch the Larry
King show, phoned in and said that it was
irrelevant whether or not Frey's story was
true: it was inspiring. Oprah Winfrey ('the
closest thing to the Zeitgeist in human
form', as Consuelo Preti writes in *Bullshit
and Philosophy*) loves the great American
storyline of degradation, realisation and
redemption. And she loves inspiration,
showing every sign of finding herself

rather inspiring. If humbug needs any justification, in other words, a large dose of inspiration supplies it.

The problem was that by using the word 'memoir' instead of 'novel' on the title page, Frey was guilty not just of humbug, but of bullshit. Now, by skewing the storyline to maximise its emotional impact, he was hiding truths. Two weeks later in a conversation with Frey on her own show, Oprah Winfrey changed tack, acknowledging (in my terms) that *A Million Little Pieces* was not an inspiring display of humbug, but bullshit. 'I made a mistake', she said, 'and I left the impression that the truth does not matter. And I am deeply sorry about that, because that is not what I believe'. (Nor do bullshitters, of course, which is why they take pains to conceal the truth.) The media frenzy was unprecedented, according to Frey's agent, Kassie Evashevski from the appropriately named Brillstein-Grey Entertainment agency. Frey's publisher accused Winfrey of being 'mean, self-serving' and 'holier-than-thou'; his agent dumped him; Riverhead reneged on a follow-up two-book deal with Frey, and 1729 readers who felt that they had been 'defrauded' by *A Million Little Pieces* received a refund from Random House.

Significantly, this fracas came to a head at a time of soaring levels of anxiety about duplicity, mostly thanks to the war in Iraq. The first few years of the twenty-first century have seen a sharpening sense in Western countries of being gulled at every level—by 'presidents, priests, politicians, lawyers, reporters, corporate executives, and countless others', just as Penny claims. This is not, however, quite the same thing as being able to aver that things are worse now than ever before in human history—or even than thirty years ago—or that 'mumbo-jumbo has conquered the world'. (An excusable bit of humbug, that title, and a hugely entertaining book.)

One of the difficulties with asserting that things are worse than they ever were is that nobody seems able to say when they were in general better, not even Penny, who has the statistics for almost anything you can think of. All the same, there is a widespread conviction among writers on

the subject that their heightened awareness of bullshit (as they usually refer to it)
is particularly appropriate at this histori-
cal juncture. The reasons they mention
cluster around the following signs of the
times: firstly, the vastly increased number
of opportunities, in comparison with any
other era, available today to scammers,
spin doctors, snake-oil salesmen, fraud-
sters and swindlers to feed the public false
information and make a buck out of doing
so; secondly, the greater sophistication,
thanks to our expanding understanding of
the workings of the human mind, of our
methods of persuasion; thirdly, the grow-
ing lack of confidence in objective truths,
the suspicion that language might not so
much reflect reality as produce it; and

fourthly, post-Enlightenment nihilism. In other words, there's a paradox at work: circumstances you might have thought would strengthen our resistance to humbug, bullshit and mindfucking, allowing us to distinguish between them and make rational choices (the abundance of information, knowing more about how the mind works, an awareness of the power of language to shape our views of the world, and freedom from medieval hocus-pocus) may well have left us vulnerable to it as never before.

Let's take these concerns one by one.

The information revolution

The amount of impersonal information available is certainly unprecedented in human history. Unless you're an Amazonian tribesman, informational isolation is an impossibility. A mere decade or so ago, if I wanted information on humpback whales, say, or Tibetan Buddhism, I went to the public library, dug about in reputable encyclopaedias, had face-to-face conversations with people I thought might know what they were talking about, and perhaps kept an eye out for articles or documentaries in the media. I can still do all of those things, of course, but my first port of call will be the Internet. Alone in my study, I have immediate access to over a million sites offering information on either of these subjects, including Wikipedia, which is not quite the same thing as the *Encyclopaedia Britannica*. From university professors to propagandists and champions of some cause or other to straight-out loonies, they're all there in front of my nose, for as long as I care to sit there, ready to speak to me in private, inform me, harangue me, threaten me, sign me up, humbug, bullshit and mindfuck me, impersonally (it's always easier to lie to someone you don't know).

We're drowning in the rising sea of information. Rather than feeling empowered by the almost infinite opportunities to know and understand, we feel weighed down by them. 'There is simply too much to think about', as Saul Bellow put it in a 1992 essay with that title. 'It is hopeless—

too many kinds of special preparation are required. In electronics, in economics, in social analysis, in history, in psychology, in international politics, most of us are, given the oceanic proliferating complexity of things, paralysed by the very suggestion that we assume responsibility for so much. This is what makes packaged opinion so attractive.' To put it another way, the flood of information is what leads us to take refuge in ideology, sound bites and clichés— they keep us afloat.

If I care to read a newspaper or two, or try the various television channels on offer in search of more information, or more objective information, or less proselytising information than the bloggers and other websites can provide, I may indeed glean a few extra nuggets from the odd documentary or news item, but I must stay alert because a mere handful of companies—all of them, from AOL Time Warner to News Corp and Disney, being broadly speaking right-wing-owned—control the global media. It's true that many of those who front the programs and write the stories have a left-wing agenda, as you would expect, but the owners have found a solution to this problem: turn information into infotainment (a form of humbug), infantilise it, restrict the news to fear, shopping and sport (actually just big business with a human face) and keep the mass of us too depressed, anxious, sullen and hooked on personality to bother informing ourselves about anything. It is now irrelevant what the world view of the presenter is—he or she might be a card-carrying Marxist, for all it matters. Deluged with stories that 'fondle the feelings and bypass the brain' (as Penny puts it), we are ripe to be not just bullshitted, but mindfucked. And we are. We don't even care any more.

In short: we can indeed arm ourselves against chicanery as never before, but the effort to do so may be leaving most of us too exhausted to bother.

The cognitive science revolution

Things were looking good for a while: the European Enlightenment led civilised peoples to believe that certain truths about the world could be deduced through reason and observation. In America they came up with 'self-evident truths', but across the Atlantic the guidelines were stricter. We did it slightly differently in different countries, with some thinkers emphasising an empirical approach, others the importance of political change away from centralised power, but the core belief was the same. A by-product of this rejection of authority and tradition, however, was the discovery that there was no 'soul', no unitary 'I', coming to freely chosen, rational decisions about what was true and what was not. Instead, the organism was the plaything of a complex set of inherited and acquired reactions to stimuli and, manipulated by those who had studied these processes, you could be made to buy or vote for virtually anything. Well, maybe *you* couldn't be, because you're smart, you're in control, but everyone else could be.

Unfortunately, the process that looked set to free us from superstition and false ideologies has left many of us with the uncomfortable suspicion that freedom itself is just a superstition. The brain now looks like just a motherboard, and not only am I not responsible for its wiring, but there is no 'I' to be responsible—for anything. I no longer have any absolute identity, the 'I' turning out to be just an eye, the self just the product of events, and character little more than an imposture.

In another paradox, then, the Enlightenment has left me open to having my wiring tampered with by any other motherboard that feels so inclined.

There is no truth

Even if you do exist, the notion that fact and fiction are indistinguishable—that the world is a parade of semblances, and reason just one discourse among many, as certain philosophers called 'postmodern' have asserted (with remarkable results in the humanities, although none in the hard sciences)—makes it difficult sometimes to work out whether you're being humbugged, bullshitted or mindfucked. Of course, unless you do use reason to determine the truth, you actually die. That's how we know that surviving postmodernists don't believe what they're teaching others to parrot: they're bullshitting them and, where they can (although it's getting harder to do), mindfucking them. If they did believe it, or the pilots flying them to their conferences did, or the engineers constructing the hotels they stay at, or the cooks working in the restaurants they eat in, or the electricians wiring their houses, or the designers of their cars, or their dentists, local chemists or taxi-drivers believed it, they'd bc dead. Yet they're not. It's as simple as that.

However, until very recently, all over the Western world, universities saw it as their duty to disgorge tens of thousands of young people every year who at the very least doubted whether there was such a thing as objective truth. You wouldn't want your own children to have these doubts, but it has been career-enhancing to encourage it in other people's children. To any fraudster, scammer, swindler or general purveyor of bullshit, this has been a boon. The humbug, for whom the show or the game is everything, is clearly in his element: life itself is a three-ring circus. For the bullshitter, for whom *a* truth is important and to be distinguished in his mind from the drivel he is massaging our feelings with, our indifference to the true/ false dichotomy is a godsend. And for the mindfucker, who may or may not believe in the revelation he is sharing with us, the market has now broadened beyond peasants and imbeciles to include an educated, well-heeled elite.

The heyday of this twaddle is now over, but the effects are still with us: Phillip Glass concerts, poems consisting of just one letter or lines such as 'ding dong / dug dirt / ditch dib / chimp chore', Federation Square, Damien Hirst, doctoral theses on Paris Hilton, and any breakfast cereal that comes in a big, cardboard box all exist because the PR industry has realised that even youngish people with money these days believe that the truth is negotiable and largely a matter of personal opinion. Nobody likes chocolate-dusted sugar bombs for breakfast more

than I do, but at least I know they're rub-
bish. I distinguish.

Nihilism

The Western world, it is argued, is largely
nihilistic today in the sense that it no
longer believes in grand truth narratives.
When that happens, people will believe, at
least temporarily, any story you spin them.
In Australia, for instance, which never had
a master text in the first place, millions fall
over themselves every year to pay homage
to a web of humbug and bullshit called 'the
Anzac story'. What other options have we
got: the history of the British monarchy?
the adventures of the Rainbow Serpent?

In the absence of grand truth narratives,
society as it was once understood ceases to

exist. Instead of the universal Church or the march of History, instead of society, we have a fun-fair array of booths hawking crystals and tales of intergalactic visitors; we have celebrity astrologers, wonder drugs, tantric Buddhism, predictions of mysterious epidemics, football frenzy and a vague fear of what Wheen calls 'secretive, impersonal forces' ruling our lives. We have been atomised. Suspended alone in a state of unrelieved apprehension bordering on panic, we cast about frenetically for some storyline to write ourselves into. Instead of citizens, we have been turned into individual consumers; instead of tradition, we have had fashion foisted on us; instead of history, we are force-fed docudramas about the mystery of the Sphinx. Desperate for company and direction, we'll form a herd behind anyone—Princess Di, JK Rowling, the Pope, Barack Obama, Lacan, anyone. Just tell us a story. It may be humbug, it may be bullshit; it doesn't matter: we don't know the difference any more. Just tell us a story. Any story. Please.

The poet Alister Kershaw didn't like the Sidney Nolan jacket design for his new book of poems one little bit. When his publisher John Reed asked him why, he said, 'I think it's shit'. 'I'm afraid, Alister,' Reed replied after a 'murderous silence', 'that you have no eye for beauty'. 'Well, that's too bad,' Kershaw countered, 'but I've got an unerring nose for shit'.

An unerring nose (eye, ear) for shit, I believe, is our best and most practical protection against the swelling tide of humbug, bullshit and mindfucking, as well as against mistaking any one of them for either of the others. Nobody in the twenty-first century can *know* very much outside a restricted field—just knowing all there is to know about chrysanthemums these days would take a lifetime, let alone mathematics, medicine, theology, sociology or philosophy. None of us can know enough about anything to be certain that somebody who knows a lot more than we do isn't misrepresenting the facts. And the world is not going to change: human beings are not going to stop humbugging, bullshitting and mindfucking; they're not going to give up trying to gull, swindle, cheat, bamboozle, dupe, defraud and hoodwink their fellow human beings for fun or profit. We are, however, it seems to me, not entirely defenceless.

Firstly, we can *care* about the truth. We can refuse to buy the argument that just because our perceptions are subjective and much of what we know is filtered through language, nothing is objectively true or knowable. We may not care whether or not it's Persil that washes whiter, but it's in our interests to be aware that something does, and through experiment or by subscribing to *Choice* magazine we can find out what it is.

Secondly, we can hone our ability to reason. If our reasoning ability breaks down in the face of the Big Questions, and we find even *A Brief History of Time* leaves us struggling, we can still use it in the face of the smaller questions, the ones that affect our lives on a daily basis. We can still protect ourselves from being constantly fooled. A respect for reason, however, doesn't mean that we can no longer take pleasure in irrationality. We can continue to indulge in humbug, for politeness and pleasure—with more finesse than ever, actually. We can still be open to revelatory experiences too, and remain alert to the promptings of intuition. It was Einstein, after all, who said that intuition was 'the only really valuable thing' and that imagination is ultimately more important than knowledge because 'knowledge is limited, whereas imagination embraces the entire world'. If, however, our default mode is reason, bullshitters will find us much harder nuts to crack.

And thirdly, like Kershaw, we can refine our nose for shit. We may never know all there is to know about the penis, for example, or whether it's the same as the phallus or the male organ, or why the impotence tonic horny goat weed complex should be expected to have any effect on its performance, but unlike Lacan as reported in the *New York Times* in 1997, we can be completely sure that a penis is not the square root of minus one. Or was that just a bit of humbug?